ECLECTUS

PARROT

Eclectus Parrot Keeping, Pros And Cons, Care, Housing, Diet And Health.

Dr. Paul Ken

Table of Contents

CHAPTER ONE

BASICS OF ECLECTUS PARROT

Charming, eye-catching, and intelligent, eclectus parrots are captivating birds that make incredible pets. Their lovely colors, talking ability, and loveable personalities have established this bird together of the foremost popular puppy parrots. This fowl is one among the larger parrot species, and it does require the right proprietor with much time and space to residence this fowl.

Species Overview

COMMON NAMES: Eclectus parrot, Solomon Island eclectus parrot, Grand eclectus parrot, yellow-sided eclectus parrot, Vosmaeri eclectus parrot, blue-bellied eclectus parrot, pink-sided eclectus parrot, dusky eclectus parrot

SCIENTIFIC NAME: Eclectus roratus

ADULT SIZE: 17 and 20 inches, weighing 13 to 18 ounces

LIFE EXPECTANCY: 30 to 50 years

ORIGIN AND HISTORY

Eclectus parrots sleep in tropical rainforests and originated within the Solomon Islands. Wild populations also stay in northeastern Australia, Indonesian, the Moluccas, and New Guinea. Its name "eclectus" springs from the word "eclectic" because the male and feminine species look so distinctive.

In their native monsoon forests, eclectus nest high within the trees. They commonly manage to seek out a deep nest hollow during a tree where they might lay their eggs and lift a circle of relatives. There are numerous eclectus parrot subspecies. The Solomon Island eclectus is that the most commonplace one within the pet trade.

TEMPERAMENT

The eclectus may be a completely friendly and intelligent chook species described as mild, tranquil, and caring. Eclectus parrots also are affectionate.

Most thrive nice while socialization may be a part of their everyday recurring. They cherish the time they spend interacting with their families. They're also touchy and should quickly grow to be pressured if they sense neglected. This fowl will learn the habitual and what to anticipate on your household. They experience the comings and goings, also as being a part of it. Around 18 months aged, the birds begin to achieve sexual maturity. Sometimes this brings with it some aggression or the intuition to "feed" something is nearby. You'll additionally notice a couple of naughty nipping behavior. This length is understood as bluffing, and its fine to disregard it and switch to distraction techniques in situ of reinforcing it. With time, they skip via the phase and research what's acceptable.

While each the ladies and men of the species make adorable pets, many homeowners claim that males have a tendency to be a touch more trainable and agreeable. On the flip side, women are often much less hooked in to their owners and usually tend to handle strain higher. Females also can be bossier and additional aggressive than a male, particularly throughout breeding. Even in captivity, a lady's nesting instincts remain strong. You would possibly find her seeking to nest in secluded regions of your home.

CHAPTER TWO

VOCALIZATION AND SPEECH

Eclectus parrots are a part of Amazons and African greys as being one among the fine species for education to talk. They're quick to research almost something you would like to show them. Many of us discover them to get on the quieter aspect when as compared to different parrots. They need an exclusive honk and other vocalizations which will be amusing the first few times, however loud and startling.

ECLECTUS PARROT COLORS AND MARKINGS

Eclectus are called sexually dimorphic, meaning that you simply may tell the sex of the fowl via its bodily characteristics. Male eclectus birds are a incredible emerald green shade with brilliant orange beaks and splashes of crimson and blue underneath their wings. Against this, the women are primarily vibrant purple with black beaks and deep crimson markings on their chests and tails. Before the first twentieth century, because the male and woman birds seemed so exceptional, they were thought to be absolutely two one-of-a-kind species. Instead of awesome lines located on many bird's feathers, eclectus feathers appear to blend. Their coloring makes for first rate camouflage of their local habitat; you'll often listen them before you'll see them.

CARING FOR AN ECLECTUS PARROT

Most eclectus birds can

stay during a multiple chicken household, however some have jealous tendencies. confirm to supply an eclectus your undivided time and interest while introducing it or any new chook or your aviary. An eclectus lives first-rate in an aviary—11 ft long through 3 foot huge and 7 feet high— especially if you hold a pair. These birds wish to fly, climb, and stay busy. If you are doing not have room for an aviary, then make sure the cage you provide is at the minimal 2 feet long by way of three ft extensive and 4 toes tall.

This species are often an honest in shape for families with kids because it features a gentle nature. However, they do not want to be startled and sort of a calm environment. They're not big fanatics of steady loud noises like barking, crying, or screaming. Thus, it is vital to recollect if your circle of relatives dynamic may be a superb healthy for the chicken.

CHAPTER THREE

COMMON HEALTH PROBLEMS

An eclectus is restricted therein it occasionally famous toe-tapping and wing-flipping. This conduct is simply like feather plucking, which may be a commonplace problem with parrots that have neglected. However, whilst all three of these actions occur in an eclectus, it is often a symbol of an intense health trouble. Nutritional deficiencies thanks to excess nutrients and minerals (like vitamin A), fortified foods, or synthetic ingredients additionally to eating foreign items like beads, or pressure are likely causes. It is vital to seem an avian vet directly.

Other health situations that an eclectus is in danger of getting include:

• Avian polyomavirus, an contamination that reasons skin tumors

• Constricted toe syndrome, a situation that causes stream to be stop to the hen's toe

• Psittacine beak and feather disease, a viral immune gadget disease

DIET AND NUTRITION

In the wild, these birds pick pomegranate, papaya, and figs, though they'll additionally devour flowers, buds on trees, and a few seeds. When saved as a pet, their food plan got to encompass fresh outcome, veggies, and carbohydrates. Cooked pasta or grain bake—a selfmade casserole only for birds—will confirm they get all the essential carbs. The eclectus features a specialized alimentary canal this is often extraordinary from many other fowl species.

This bird desires to be fed a eating regimen high in fiber and low in fat. It's additionally pleasant to stay far away from too many vitamin and mineral supplements, which could cause digestive tumors or abnormal behavior. Avoid feeding parrot mixes that contain artificial dyes, flavorings, or preservatives. These additives could cause your pet to lose its lovely color and may even be poisonous for this touchy species. An eclectus' day by day meal should be approximately eighty percent outcome and vegetables—the rest are

often parrot pellets. Give seeds
and nuts as occasional treats.
Feed this bird twice each day,
once   upon   rising,   and   1 to
2 hours before bedtime. Offer 1
cup of culmination and greens
and 1/three cup of parrot blend
at   every   feeding.

CHAPTER FOUR

EXERCISE

The eclectus are active birds and wants many rooms to exercise. They need to have access to an enormous play stand and hen-safe vicinity for hiking and exploring. At the very least, offer an hour of free flight time before breakfast and another hour of loose flight time before dinner.

You'll additionally get to provide these birds many perches of various materials and diameters, so their toes still are healthy. A mountaineering ladder swings, and a slew of amusing toys to beat up and chew on can even make the eclectus happy. If furnished with enough stimulation, they are doing a far better activity than many parrots at keeping themselves occupied when you are not around. The greater challenges you'll supply these clever birds, the higher.

Pros

• Social, affectionate, and loves attention

• Intelligent, generally, an amazing speakme parrot

- Quieter parrot than the various speakme species

• Needs an aviary or large cage to thrive

• doesn't like chaotic environments or steady loud sounds

WHERE TO ADOPT OR BUY AN ECLECTUS PARROT

Potential proprietors need to spend time with several exceptional birds, if possible, to seek out the one with an identical personality. Eclectus parrots aren't as commonplace as

22

others,   so you'll also shall checking out out a specialty pet store or breeder. On average, breeders promote eclectus parrots from $1,000 to $3,000. Online rescues, adoption organizations, and breeders where you'll find eclectus parrots encompass:

- Adopt a Pet
- Hookbills purchasable
- Bird Breeders

Look for a bird that's vibrant, alert, and lively. Make positive the breeder is informed approximately their birds and is forthcoming about their breeding practices and therefore the origin of their birds. They need to provide you with with helpful facts for elevating eclectus parrots and tell you about the fowl are a day habitual.

THE END